FOSSIL FILES

INSECT
FOSSILS

BARBARA M. LINDE

PowerKiDS
press™

NEW YORK

Published in 2017 by The Rosen Publishing Group, Inc.
29 East 21st Street, New York, NY 10010

First Edition

Editor: Melissa Raé Shofner
Book Design: Tanya Dellaccio

Photo Credits: Cover, p. 11 MarcelClemens/Shutterstock.com; cover, back cover, p.1 Victoria Kalinina/Shutterstock.com; p. 5 AlessandroZocc/Shutterstock.com; p. 7 (fly) irin-k/Shutterstock.com; p. 7 (ant fossil) Schellhorn/ullstein bild/Getty Images; pp. 9 (cockroach fossil), 25 (water beetle) Colin Keates/Getty Images; p. 9 (microscope) https://commons.wikimedia.org/wiki/File:Hooke-microscope.png; p. 13 feathercollector/Shutterstock.com; p. 13 (viburnum fossil) https://commons.wikimedia.org/wiki/File:ViburnumFossil.jpg; p. 15 (fungus gnat) Bjoern Wylezich/Shutterstock.com; p. 15 (midge) Matteo Chinellato/Shutterstock.com; p. 16 Alexander Chelmodeev/Shutterstock.com; p. 17 Eddie Gerald/Getty Images; p. 19 tobkatrina/Shutterstock.com; p. 21 (cicada fossil) Pan Xunbin/Shutterstock.com; p. 21 (cicada) Steve Byland/Shutterstock.com; p. 23 (*Meganeura* illustration) De Agostini Picture Library/De Agostini/Getty Images; p. 23 CM Dixon/Print Collector/Getty Images; p. 25 (La Brea Tar Pits) Romans_1_20/Shutterstock.com; p. 27 Bradley Allen Murrell/Shutterstock.com.

Library of Congress Cataloging-in-Publication Data

Names: Linde, Barbara M.
Title: Insect fossils / Barbara M. Linde.
Description: New York : PowerKids Press, [2017] | Series: Fossil files | Includes index.
Identifiers: LCCN 2016041762| ISBN 9781499427448 (pbk. book) | ISBN 9781508152705 (6 pack) | ISBN 9781499428605 (library bound book)
Subjects: LCSH: Insects, Fossil–Juvenile literature. | Fossils–Juvenile literature.
Classification: LCC QE831 .L56 2017 | DDC 565/.7–dc23
LC record available at https://lccn.loc.gov/2016041762

Manufactured in the United States of America

CPSIA Compliance Information: Batch Batch #BW17PK: For Further Information contact Rosen Publishing, New York, New York at 1-800-237-9932

CONTENTS

ANCIENT INSECTS

When you think about fossils, dinosaurs or woolly mammoths probably come to mind—not insects. After all, it's hard to imagine a **fragile** moth wing being preserved in stone. Insect fossils do exist, though, and it's very exciting to find one.

Insects existed on Earth millions of years before dinosaurs. Unfortunately, they're less likely to be preserved than creatures with bones or many hard body parts. However, even tiny mosquitoes have been found trapped in amber for millions of years.

Scientists have made amazing insect fossil discoveries all over the world. There are a few places on Earth where conditions are just right for preserving fragile insect remains. We can learn a lot about Earth's past by studying insect fossils today.

This prehistoric insect fossil may be millions of years old.

Dig It!

When most plants and animals die, their bodies break down and disappear. Only a few of the millions of plants and animals that lived in the past have turned into fossils.

WHAT IS AN INSECT?

There are more than 1 million species, or kinds, of insects on Earth. They come in many shapes and sizes, but there are a few things they all have in common. Insects have three body segments, or parts: the head, thorax, and abdomen. The mouthparts, eyes, and a pair of antennae are on an insect's head. One or two pairs of wings and six legs are attached to the thorax, or middle section. The abdomen is behind the thorax. The abdomen holds the stomach, intestines, and other organs.

Insects are invertebrates. This means they don't have a backbone. Instead, they have a hard outer covering called an exoskeleton. An exoskeleton is a protective shell. Insect larvae, or babies, hatch from eggs. Larvae usually look much different than adult insects.

Dig It!

Ants are insects. They're actually related to wasps. Worker ants don't have wings, but males and females that mate do.

Parts of a Fly

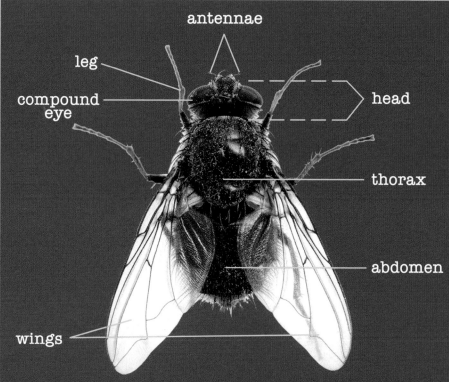

antennae

leg

compound
eye

head

thorax

abdomen

wings

Do you see two antennae, six legs, and three body segments? If so, you're looking at an insect.

STUDYING INSECT FOSSILS

Paleontology is the study of fossils. By studying fossils, scientists called paleontologists are able to learn more about the history of our planet. They try to figure out why some plants and animals died while others adapted and survived. Fossils help scientists learn about the climate, atmosphere, and diseases of long ago.

Earth has been constantly changing for billions of years. Many species no longer exist today because they couldn't adapt fast enough or well enough. However, some ancient creatures were able to evolve, or change over time. Their **descendants** are alive today. Cockroaches are a great example. Early roaches first appeared on Earth around 350 million years ago. Whatever killed off the dinosaurs 65 million years ago was no match for these insects. Cockroaches are true survivors.

Early Ideas About Fossils

In the mid-1600s, an English scientist named Robert Hooke invented a new type of microscope. He used his new microscope to look at fossils and compare them with the plants and animals of his time. He became certain that fossils were the remains of ancient plants and animals. Hooke was the first person to use a microscope to examine fossils. He also figured out how fossils formed. Hooke's ideas and methods changed the way other scientists worked.

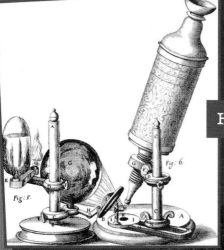

Hooke's microscope

Scientists believe this early cockroach once lived in warm, damp forests. Cockroaches can be found in similar **environments** today.

WHAT IS A FOSSIL?

Most ancient insects were eaten by other animals or simply died and rotted away. However, some were preserved as fossils. A body fossil may be the whole body of an insect or another organism. It could also be part of an organism, such as an insect's exoskeleton, jaws, or wings. A trace fossil shows something about how an organism moved or lived. Tail or wing tracks are trace insect fossils. A preserved leaf that contains bite marks from an insect is also a trace fossil.

Insect fossils are storytellers from the past. From them, we learn about the size and shape of insects that lived long ago. We can tell what they ate and what ate them. Insect fossils may also give us clues about what the environment used to be like.

Dig It!

Entomology is the study of insects. Scientists who study insect fossils are called paleoentomologists.

Scientists studying 50-million-year-old fossils discovered that prehistoric crickets had ears on their front legs below their knees. Nearly **identical** ears can be found on crickets living today.

SAVED BY SEDIMENT

Sediment is sand, rocks, and other bits of materials that are moved by wind, water, or ice. The sediment gets **deposited** in layers. The oldest layers of sediment are on the bottom, and the newest are on the top.

Ancient insects sometimes became trapped in sediment. Sometimes parts of an insect's body, such as its exoskeleton or wings, were preserved. Sometimes an insect's body rotted away but left a mold of its shape. Water flowing through the sediment carried minerals, such as **quartz**, which filled in the shape of the insect. The minerals then hardened and created a cast in the exact shape of the insect. Insect trails, larva cases, and nests have been preserved as trace fossils.

Dig It!

The word "fossil" comes from the Latin word *fossilis*, which means "dug up."

This leaf fossil shows bite marks from prehistoric insects.

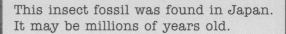
This insect fossil was found in Japan. It may be millions of years old.

TRAPPED IN AMBER

Some trees produce a sticky liquid called resin. When a tree's bark is damaged, resin seeps out. Resin then hardens to protect the tree. Thanks to resin, we can study the fossilized bodies of many ancient insects.

Sometimes an insect landed in sticky resin. Other times, resin dripped onto an insect resting on a tree trunk. Either way, the insect became stuck. The resin covered the insect and hardened in the air and sunlight. The piece of hardened resin dropped to the ground. Over time, it was buried under layers of soil and sometimes water. Eventually, the resin turned into clear, hard, golden-colored amber. The entire body of an insect may be perfectly preserved in amber for millions of years.

This fossilized insect is called a fungus gnat. It's been preserved in amber.

close-up of a midge in amber

Paleontologists find out a lot from insects trapped in amber. One piece of amber held an ant and bits of leaves. This gave scientists clues about what the ant ate. Another piece of amber held two ants that appeared to be fighting. Scientists discovered that they were two different species of ants.

Scientists working in the Alps in northeastern Italy in 2012 discovered a tiny fly and two **mites** preserved in amber. The mites belonged to two species that had never been seen before. Scientists believe these three little creatures lived about 230 million years ago. That makes the tiny fly more than 100 million years older than any other insect found in amber so far. Paleontologists realized that insects have been around for much longer than they first thought.

If these ants aren't careful, they may become stuck in the nearby resin. They could be preserved in amber for millions of years.

Fossils for Fun and Profit

Many fossils are beautiful and interesting. It's no wonder that many people collect them. Some people buy, sell, and trade fossils for profit. Amber, with or without preserved organisms inside, is often used to make jewelry. Furniture and buildings are sometimes made from stones that have fossils in them. Fossilized wood is also used to make furniture. Groups of fossil collectors meet in person or online. There are websites just for fossil collectors.

THE OLDEST INSECT FOSSIL

In the 1920s, paleontologists found a tiny fossil in Scotland. It was so small that they couldn't see it clearly, even with a microscope. They put it away in a drawer in a London museum. In 2002, a scientist took another look at the fossil using a more powerful microscope. He saw a **miniature** pair of insect jaws.

When scientists dated this insect fossil, they found out it was about 400 million years old. It's the oldest insect fossil discovered so far. Scientists compared the jaws to those of other winged insect fossils. The jaws shared similar features. Before this find, scientists thought that the first winged insects developed about 320 million years ago. Now they knew that insects developed wings much earlier.

This piece of amber contains 10-million-year-old mosquitoes. Scientists now know that insects developed wings hundreds of millions of years before these mosquitoes lived.

CICADA FOSSILS

On a warm summer evening, you might hear buzzing and clicking noises in your backyard. These may be made by male cicadas. Cicadas are large insects. They live everywhere except Antarctica.

Some fossils show that early cicadas were much larger than those alive today. Others show how cicada wings evolved. Later cicadas could fly higher and faster. One type of prehistoric cicada didn't have the body parts that let them make noise. Scientists know that cicadas developed this ability over time.

In 2011, scientists discovered the oldest fossilized cicada. The cicada had been trapped in amber. It had legs like those of modern cicadas. Before this find, scientists thought cicadas first appeared around 40 million years ago. This fossil proved that cicadas existed about 110 million years ago.

Giant cicadas lived during the Jurassic and Cretaceous periods. Paleontologists thought they were butterflies when their fossils were first discovered.

modern cicada

WHAT A SITE!

The Elmo fossil site in Elmo, Kansas, contains a huge number of insect fossils from about 300 million to 250 million years ago. It's dry land now, but the area was once a swampy forest with a large lake nearby.

Most of the fossils found at Elmo are small. However, scientists did find a fossil of what is possibly the largest insect ever. *Meganeuropsis* was a griffinfly, which was a relative of the modern dragonfly. Most dragonflies today have a wingspan of about 2 to 5 inches (5.1 to 12.7 cm). *Meganeuropsis* had a wingspan of 29 inches (73.7 cm). It was found in 1939, and it's still the largest insect fossil ever discovered. From this fossil, we know for sure that some insects were once much larger than they are today.

Dig It!

Paleontologists first found fossils at the Elmo site in 1899. They included some of the oldest fossils found at that time.

This fossilized dragonfly is
from the Jurassic period.
It's between 201 million
and 145 million years old.

STICKY TAR PITS

Some places around the world have large pits of tar. Ancient animals, including insects, often got trapped in this sticky stuff. The tar preserved whole animals as well as body parts. By studying fossils found in tar pits, paleontologists learn which animals ate insects and which insects ate other animals. Fossils also help scientists figure out the time periods when insect-eating animals lived.

Tar pits usually have a shallow covering of water. It's possible that insects tried to land on the water and got stuck in the tar. Hungry carnivores trying to reach the insects also got trapped. It's also possible the larger animals became stuck first and died in the tar. When flies and beetles landed on their bodies for a meal, they also became trapped.

Beetles and Bones

In 2013, scientists at the La Brea Tar Pits in Los Angeles, California, found traces of beetle larvae on the fossilized bones of large herbivores. From these traces, scientists learned that the beetle larvae fed on the bones. They also figured out what the climate was like when the animals died. Scientists determined that it took between 17 and 20 weeks for the animals to fully sink into the tar.

This water beetle fossil is about 1.8 million years old. It was found preserved in a tar pit.

La Brea Tar Pits

BARSTOW BUGS

The 19-million-year-old Barstow Formation is a fossil hunter's dream. It's part of the Rainbow Basin near Barstow, California. Although it's in a desert now, it used to be a lake bed with plenty of water and nearby trees. It's an excellent place to find fossils. Part of the site is called Fossil Canyon. The insect fossils found here are sometimes called "Barstow bugs."

The way sediment piled up in this area is unusual. The insect fossils here are well preserved and easy to remove. Lumps of sediment may be soaked in acid to reveal the quartz insect fossils inside. Paleontologists can study whole preserved insects, not just flat imprints or parts. They've even found colors on some fossils. This may be the only place on Earth with fossils like these.

Dig It!

October 14 of every year is National Fossil Day in the United States. The National Park Service has preserved many fossil sites all over the country.

Rainbow Basin is in the Mojave Desert. The site is filled with fossils, but you need a permit to remove them from the area.

PREHISTORIC BLOOD

In 2013, a scientist examining insect fossils at the National Museum of Natural History noticed the unusually dark abdomen of a fossilized mosquito. Using special **X-rays** and other tests, a team of scientists found blood in the mosquito's stomach. It's not clear which ancient animal the blood is from, but it isn't dinosaur blood. Still, the blood is an amazing find. It's the first time blood has ever been found inside a fossilized insect. Now scientists know for sure that blood can be preserved in fossils. They're studying the fossil to learn more about ancient blood-sucking insects.

This find also proved that mosquitoes were alive around 46 million years ago. This is much earlier than scientists first thought.

Dig It!

The Kishenehn Formation is in northwestern Montana. The **shale** rock from the bottom of a dried-up lake bed there holds many insect fossils from about 46 million years ago.

INSECT FOSSIL TIMELINE

TIME PERIOD	MILLIONS OF YEARS AGO	COMMON INSECTS
DEVONIAN	419–359	insects without wings: springtails, bristletails
CARBONIFEROUS	359–299	first winged insects: mayflies, grasshoppers, cockroaches
PERMIAN	299–252	beetles, flies, booklice
TRIASSIC	252–201	dragonflies, wasps, stick insects
JURASSIC	201–145	earwigs, moths, butterflies
CRETACEOUS	145–66	termites, fleas, ants
PALEOGENE	66–23	praying mantises, bees

Earth's history is divided into time periods. Fossils tell us which insects first developed during which time period.

THE SEARCH GOES ON

Would you like to become a paleontologist? If so, then study hard now and plan to go to college. Take lots of biology courses, including plant and animal **anatomy**. Learn about geology and earth science and study evolution. You may want to volunteer at a natural history museum.

Paleontologists continue to study fossils that have already been found. They use new **technology** to get more detailed information. They also keep finding new fossil sites. They create new databases filled with facts and figures. Thanks to the Internet, scientists around the world can share their work almost instantly. Their hard work gives us a better understanding of how life has evolved on Earth. Perhaps you'll join them someday.

GLOSSARY

anatomy: The study of the structure of the body.

deposit: To let fall or sink.

descendant: An animal that comes from an animal of an earlier time.

fragile: Delicate and easily broken.

environment: The conditions that surround a living thing and affect the way it lives.

identical: Exactly the same.

miniature: On a smaller scale.

mite: A tiny member of the spider family.

quartz: A very hard kind of rock.

shale: Rock that is made of hardened mud or clay.

technology: A method that uses science to solve problems and the tools used to solve those problems.

X-ray: A powerful type of energy that is similar to light but is invisible to the human eye.

INDEX

WEBSITES

Due to the changing nature of Internet links, PowerKids Press has developed an online list of websites related to the subject of this book. This site is updated regularly. Please use this link to access the list: www.powerkidslinks.com/ff/insct